DIVORCE WITH CIVILITY

A private, dignified and cost efficient way to exit a broken marriage

By Attorney Ann C. LoDolce

Mediator and Family Law Attorney

ISBN: 978-0-578-02783-8

About the Author

Ann C. LoDolce has been a practicing attorney for over 34 years, with a primary emphasis in family law matters. She is AV rated, the highest ethical and professional peer review designation. Even in divorce litigation, her philosophy is settlement orientated. Armed with a laptop computer and portable printer at all times, Attorney LoDolce is known to continually promote settlement even after trial has commenced. Concern for the client's financial, emotional and physical well being is always her primary focus. It is this concern that has encouraged her to explore all forms of divorce resolution.

Attorney LoDolce earned her Juris Doctorate from Suffolk University Law School in 1974, a Master of Arts from the University of Connecticut in 1968, and a Bachelor of Science from Skidmore College in 1966. A former associate college law professor, she has been on the faculty for family law courses sponsored by the Massachusetts Continuing Legal Education, Inc. and the Massachusetts Bar Association, both of which promote continuing legal education for lawyers. For ten years, Attorney LoDolce was the chairperson of the Southeastern Regional Bench Bar Committee, which acts as a liaison between judges and attorneys to improve the Probate Court system.

Attorney LoDolce resides with her husband of 34 years and they have two children. Her practice, LoDolce Family Law, includes Plymouth, Norfolk and Bristol Counties. Additional information may be obtained at www.lodolcefamilylaw.com or by calling 508-583-2424.

Definitions

Mediation. Mediation is one type of dispute resolution in which the participants meet with a trained neutral person, a mediator, in order to work through their issues. These meetings typically occur outside the presence of attorneys. After each session, a mediator will usually issue a written summary of what was accomplished, which can then be forwarded to the parties' respective attorneys for review and input.

A mediator does not take sides or represent the interests of either party but moderates the discussions between the parties, often making non-binding suggestions. The participants retain control over the process and therefore the results. The driving force behind mediation is the motivation to settle at a controlled cost in a controlled setting. Occasionally, the mediator will work in tandem with a psychologist or various other combinations of professionals in order to help the parties move effectively toward settlement.

Interactive Mediation. Interactive Mediation is a similar process but one that includes the participation of attorneys in the mediation sessions. Often attorneys will first prepare a summary of the case for the mediator, which saves time and effectively brings the mediator up to speed on the unresolved aspects of the divorce. For example, it is entirely possible for parties to have resolved the matter of custody but not visitation, or to have resolved all matters concerning the children but not those pertaining to the division of the marital property.

An interactive mediator may be an attorney or a retired judge. The interactive mediator may make non-binding suggestions and although the parties still retain control over the results, the mediator is an active participant as well as a moderator.

Collaborative Law. Collaborative Law is another option for alternative dispute resolution and consists of a team approach where the parties and their collaboratively trained attorneys come together with a collaboratively trained mental health professional referred to as a "divorce coach." The divorce coach acts as a neutral person and encourages civility while guiding the group dynamics toward settlement. The team can consist of any number of professionals such as financial advisors or children's counselors depending on the particular needs of the individual case. The theory behind this process is to provide the participants with all necessary resources to promote a comprehensive divorce settlement. Typically, prior to beginning the process, the parties agree that they will not seek court intervention while participating in a collaborative forum, but will go to court only at the end in order to have their agreement approved by the judge. If at some point during the process negotiations break down and the parties choose to litigate their divorce, their attorneys must withdraw from the case and the parties must find new counsel.

Litigation. Litigation is a process where one or both parties ("litigants") file a court complaint to give a judge the authority to resolve family disputes. The judge is either appointed by the Governor or an elected official who, after hearing each point of view, makes a decision. If the hearing is for a limited portion of the dispute, then that hearing may result in what is referred to as a "temporary order." While the hearing itself may only last for five minutes, the effects of the resulting order may be far reaching, determining such things as the amount of support to be paid, where the children will live, or even whether or not one litigant should be mandated to leave the home. Temporary orders often influence what a judge will ultimately issue as a final order. If the hearing or trial is scheduled for the entire matter, then both parties will have an opportunity to present their entire story or "case," along with witnesses who may testify on a variety of matters such as the value of assets, the ability of a litigant to have custody of the children, or events that occurred during the marriage.

Since the courts are typically understaffed and over-booked, many hours are frequently lost while litigants wait to be called. At any time during the wait for a hearing, a litigant has the right to pursue mediation or engage in settlement discussions. Litigation can be very expensive since many hours of preparation are required prior to a court hearing and family law attorneys are paid by the hour. Litigation is also stressful for the participants since the outcome is solely dependant upon the judge's impressions gleaned from what is presented in a structured and often limited hearing. The judge's picture of the relationship of the parties is obtained from a small lens, and the judgment or decision often fails to resolve problems to the satisfaction of both litigants. In fact, a good decision is often said to be one in which both parties are somewhat unhappy. A judge has wide discretion and unless a decision is found to be seriously flawed by legal standards, it is typically not appealable.

And with appeals, the process only becomes more expensive and time consuming with limited promise of success.

By litigating, parties grant a stranger the authority to make even the most basic decisions about their family. Frequently, a divorce will start with litigation but will end by way of a negotiated settlement, either with or without mediation. Few family law disputes are resolved by a full trial. However, even when a judge enters only one or two temporary orders prior to a matter settling, such orders have the ability to significantly limit the final outcome. Retaining control over the process from start to finish through alternative dispute resolution is optimal. Of course, in a case where the parties refuse to agree, litigation must continue to be available and there are those situations, where there is abuse for example, when litigation remains the only option.

Introduction

Divorce with civility starts with a state of mind. Civility is helpful whether pursuing a litigated divorce or a resolution by way of alternative methods. A healthy, productive state of mind is crucial in allowing parties to get through the process as comfortably as possible, no matter which means of resolution is selected. Some divorces clearly need to be litigated, and having practiced divorce litigation for thirty-four years, I assure you that an attorney's ability to try a case is an essential skill. When filing a divorce action in the courts, a party and his or her counsel must be willing and able to go to trial if need be. With that said, alternative dispute resolution has recently become more available and warrants serious consideration given that most divorces can, with the appropriate guidance, be resolved absent a full trial. While my office continues to offer all forms of representation, it has become increasingly apparent that the benefits of civility no matter what form of representation is sought will make the process easier, less expensive and less painful for all concerned.

This is not a "how to" book but an exploration of a state of mind needed to proceed with dignity by exercising civility to one another, the children, the attorneys and the court. This positive approach does not encourage a blind acceptance of any proposal, but provides reasonable and dignified ways in which parties can interact during settlement negotiations with a final divorce settlement as the objective.

Options for pursuing a civil divorce can include the employment of alternative divorce resolution such as mediation or collaborative law. Although alternative divorce resolution may generate the very same result as if the divorce were litigated, the *process* will undeniably cost the parties far less, financially and emotionally. Time, money, and energy will not be unnecessarily expended on multiple court hearings. The journey will be less wearing on all, and in the end more conducive to the possibility of the parties' interpersonal relationship surviving, albeit in a new way; a notion worthy of consideration particularly if children are involved.

The goal of a civil divorce whether through mediation or collaborative law is to employ an acceptable process for the purpose of ending an unacceptable relationship. Where there are children, a divorce marks the beginning of a new relationship established in order to meet the future needs of those children. Even with adult children, the divorced parents are expected to interact at major events such as weddings, holidays and religious celebrations. If a divorce is achieved with civility, these later events can transpire more comfortably. By adopting a positive approach to the divorce process and embracing a cloak of reasonableness, the results can be far reaching, dictating how otherwise warring parties will interact not only throughout the process but for many years to follow.

This book is based on the experiences of more than three decades of practicing matrimonial law. As a result of my interactions with couples and attorneys in the divorce arena, I have come to believe that a divorce need not poison the emotional well being of the parties and that mediation is one of the best ways to avoid such toxic results. While this book is by no means intended to offer a scientific formula for divorce resolution, it is a candid reflection after years on the inside track. It is my hope that such disclosure may encourage those faced with an impending divorce to consider a more humane way to travel down that difficult road. It is my firm belief that the by-products of a civilized divorce benefit all involved; the participants, their children, and the attorneys, delivering a better quality of life for all.

No matter how you slice it, the process of divorcing is complicated. There simply is no easy answer or quick escape given that a marriage consists of a life merger between two individuals, in which unique histories and personalities are intertwined. For a marriage to work in the first place, parties must be able to successfully merge all of their "stuff" irrespective of what that may entail. Although there is always a tendency to point fingers at the commencement of a divorce action, I have found that there is usually sufficient blame to go around and that everyone, without fail, brings issues, problems, and hang-ups to the marital table.

In fact, I believe that the key to a successful marriage is for the parties to have compatible neuroses. One's flaws and foibles should be known far before the marriage occurs, perhaps by way of premarital counseling, allowing the parties to become genuinely familiar with one another. Such a proactive step would help avoid that sense of disillusionment that commonly results when there are unattainable expectations based on a genuine lack of understanding. People need to be realistic. They need to identify the negative personality traits going into the marriage and honestly reflect upon whether those traits are acceptable.

The fact is that it is more intuitive for courting couples to focus on the positive traits and habits of their partners as they head down the aisle, choosing to ignore all of the less attractive bits and pieces. It could be argued, according to divorce statistics, that at least half of those entering a marriage are doing so without a sincere understanding of their future spouses; this of course leads to the disappointment and unhappiness that often precedes a divorce action.

The single greatest cause of divorce is incivility, which is the knee-jerk reaction to the unavoidable disappointment resulting from the lofty and unachievable expectations placed on a marriage. The cascade of uncivil, inappropriate behavior eventually becomes codified within the family interaction. One party's discourtesy feeds off the other's, the children mimic their parents, and bit by bit, everyone's behavior disintegrates on a daily basis until the marriage is over and all involved have lost their way; small wonder that anyone could remain in such a state for very long. The reality is that many people consider marriage to be a license to behave badly. The fallout of this counterproductive communication and lack of consideration is that people are getting divorced at an alarmingly rapid rate, and many young couples understandably fail to see the merit of getting married at all, preferring to live together rather than committing to an institution noted for its tremendous rate of failure.

Frequently, once a decision has been made to divorce, the common and unfortunate progression is for the communication between the parties to quickly become contentious and acrimonious. While no two divorces are any more alike than any two marriages, it is the difficult divorces on which this book will focus.

Lastly, the recommendations made in this book for civil negotiations are based on an assumption that no domestic violence exists in the marriage. When a spouse is in physical danger, the normal channels of sitting down to resolve marital disputes are not available to the parties as the escalation of the dispute could result in a dangerous or possibly life threatening situation. If such a level of acrimony exists, any and all negotiations need to be without personal interaction and with the assistance of trained third parties such as attorneys, court mediators and judges, ideally in a neutral setting such as the courthouse where court officers are also close-by to lend assistance if needed.

Anecdotes and examples in this book have been modified so not to identify the fact patterns of actual cases in which I have been involved and to protect the identity of all clients, past and present. Any similarities that may exist to real life persons or events are strictly coincidental.

March 2010
Ann C. LoDolce

Dedication

The practice of family law is challenging at best. Without the support of Elaine Epstein, Kerry Curnow, Jean Nunes and Michael Wayshak, I would not be able to meet these daily challenges. To them I dedicate this book.

Chapter I

Why Be Civil in a Divorce?

What is divorce with civility? With fifty percent of all marriages failing, divorce is undeniably commonplace. At the same time, divorce can be one of the most horrific experiences one may ever encounter. Because of the potential for emotional and financial devastation by way of a litigated divorce, it only makes sense to explore kinder means of resolution and to commit to making the process less painful and less taxing for all involved.

Uncivil divorces commonly consist of bad behavior from start to finish, including yelling, interrupting and belittling, all in an attempt to endorse irrational positions. Some promote ill will by using the children to relay messages, to request money or to manipulate the other party. In the worst cases, some will encourage the alienation of a child from the other parent in order to better position themselves for an impending custody battle, seeking financial advantage by way of preferential footholds. Others perpetuate bad faith by manufacturing false claims either in retaliation or to somehow gain the upper hand. And of course many attempt to conceal assets that require disclosure in order for the divorce to be appropriately resolved.

By choosing to behave in any of the above ways is to consciously allow a divorce to take on a life of its own, taking the focus away from those issues that are in dire need of attention: the needs of the children, the disposition of assets, the ability to survive financially post divorce, where the parties will live, with whom the children will live, how the family medical and dental expenses will be paid, and how a surviving parent and the children will be cared for should one parent die. At best, the task is daunting; there is no time for unproductive arguing or juvenile jockeying. Lives will be restructured by the divorce; there is no avoiding it. However, if people choose to meaningfully participate in the process they will retain far more control on the outcome and the future of their families.

The less a party is able to behave in an appropriate, civil manner, the more the individual ultimately forfeits the opportunity to productively participate in bringing his or her divorce to resolution. When a participant proceeds with civility, the right to make life decisions is retained rather than placing it in the hands of a third party; a judge who receives select information and makes a decision based on that limited information. It is as if the judge looks though a key hole of the door to a large room and is then expected to accurately describe the valuable pieces of art hanging on each and every wall. It is simply impossible. A judge's decision is not perfect. Of course the advantage of having a judge make a decision is that it gets done. Yet, even after a judgment has entered and a divorce is final, the unresolved emotional issues that a court cannot resolve remain firmly in place, often with far reaching tentacles capable of impacting the lives of generations to follow. An attorney practicing for decades, for example, may represent multiple generations of family members who remarkably present with very similar marital problems. To add insult to injury, when a judge hears any aspect of a divorce, those hearings usually occur in a public courtroom where the veneer of privacy and dignity is non-existent. Mediation offers a viable alternative to all of this.

The fever pitch commonly associated with the divorce process can become so heated that individuals often waive their rights to participate effectively in the process, largely without realizing the consequences of their angry misbehavior. The courts cope with this problem in a variety of ways: court officers being asked to separate arguing parties in the courthouse building itself, leaving the attorneys in a separate area to negotiate on behalf of their clients; police officers being called upon to assist normally rational adults who simply cannot interact appropriately even for the seconds it takes to drop off or pick up their children; and courts entering orders *prohibiting* verbal exchanges between the parties in the presence of their children. It is amazing that in a world that is so focused on communication via every possible medium such as e-mail, texting and twittering to name a few, people in the divorce arena regularly and voluntarily relinquish the right to express themselves at all, simply because they refuse to do so in a respectful and productive manner.

The lack of civility that caused a marriage to break down in the first place often increases exponentially during the course of a litigated divorce, frequently resulting in emotional and financial devastation for the parties. Everyone suffers; everyone is targeted, including the children, those unwitting beneficiaries of the bad behavior of "grownups." Otherwise intelligent, loving, and responsible parents willingly and regularly exhibit such hostility and inappropriate behavior in the presence of their children that there cannot help but be indelible emotional marks sustained by these children; marks that they will likely pass on to the next generation, all because the disease of incivility has taken hold.

While this lack of civility is truly an indictment of our society where people typically treat strangers on the street with a greater degree of civility than that extended to their own spouses or children, the challenge here is to adopt one consistent code of conduct, irrespective of whether speaking to the attorney, the soon to be ex-spouse, the client, opposing counsel or the judge. Years of divorce practice, not to mention pure logic, would suggest that the same results can be reached far more quickly, less painfully and less expensively simply by choosing to behave in a courteous manner.

Merits of the institution of marriage. Marriage, whether by way of a religious codification or a civil ceremony, has long been the foundation of our society. The institution of marriage is one that continues to persevere despite the sobering statistics of failed attempts and is equally cherished by those for whom such a union has only recently become available, the gay community. So long as marriage continues to be valued, the reality of divorce remains.

Rancor. It is impossible to quantify the tremendous pain associated with a divorce or the communication blockages created by feelings of betrayal and how all of this impedes individuals' abilities to amicably resolve disputes. However, if armed with the appropriate tools, it is possible to consider designing a graceful exit strategy. The heart of this concept relies on appropriate behavior, better communication and a commitment to implement a better process.

Civility has to be preferential to the rancor and tension from which people typically suffer while in the midst of a litigated divorce. Such rancor can elevate to the point where court personnel and attorneys are on notice with respect to potentially dangerous scenarios. In one probate and family courthouse, for example, where there is an open floor plan and multiple levels, court officers are often instructed to maintain a visible presence in the atrium area where one disgruntled party may be tempted to push the other over a balcony. The film, *War of the Roses*, while ostensibly fiction, is an apt portrayal of the tension and pain people often experience during the process of divorce. But it does not need to be this way.

There are some who, while in the throes of a divorce, are able to sit down and talk out their issues, not for the purpose of reconciling but in order to devise a plan to sufficiently divide their property and settle their financial and custodial issues. The common denominators in these cases are productive communication and a desire to simply end the wrangling. Most often, however, this "settlement" occurs in the eleventh hour at a time when the divorce is about to go to trial and the parties are finally motivated to put an end to the litigation because if they don't, the judge will, and only after both parties have incurred substantially increased legal fees. Often by this time, the parties are not only financially depleted, but have also exhausted most of their emotional capital. This type of collaboration does not need to stem from financial and emotional desperation but can be chosen at the onset of a divorce action.

Resolution. Mediation offers a process in which the parties meet in a private place to discuss personal and financial problems for the purpose of resolution. When in court, it is not uncommon to wait several hours until a case is called, then days, weeks or even months until a decision is rendered, during which time problems often only fester. With some foresight and a commitment to purpose, this resolution can occur long before the parties are depleted financially and otherwise. Although it may be difficult to fully comprehend the benefit of early settlement, the rewards are plentiful; the emotional strain is lessened, the financial burden reduced, and people are given the opportunity to keep their dignity intact while working through tremendously taxing and personal issues.

Mediation requires a willingness to follow some fundamental ground rules: everyone is committed to staying focused on the agenda at hand; the parties are respectful of others at all times; and everyone does his or her very best to keep calm no matter how emotional the topics become. If the parties cannot do this on their own or with the help of legal counsel, a trained mediator or divorce coach may be retained in order to facilitate the process. Above all else, the parties must continually remind themselves that effective communication is the key to moving successfully through the process.

The option of divorce resolution is not a new concept, but given that litigation is largely chosen despite the availability of mediation, it can only be assumed that people are either skeptical about the probability of success through mediation, or for whatever reason are not yet ready to end the fighting. The divorce process has a rhythm of its own and people need time to adjust to the changes in their lives. People often experience the same stages of grief during the course of a divorce as when a loved one dies: denial, anger, bargaining, depression and finally acceptance. But even after people have accepted the circumstances for what they are, when the fight surely should be over, in many instances the war manages to wage on...and on… and on. In such a case, incivility becomes a bad habit, much like road rage where there is an unhealthy, unthinking default response. People must demand better, more of themselves and more for their loved ones; choosing civil behavior is a way to avoid knee-jerk toxic responses, not only to improve interfamilial relations, but to better serve their own interests in obtaining a divorce at less of a financial and emotional cost.

Chapter II

Marriage Contract: Before and After the Fall

A marriage between two people is a merger of two families with two sets of traditions, histories, and practices and is sometimes a melding of different cultural and religious belief systems. People who marry bring with them the "baggage" of their family experiences and prior relationships and/or previous marriages. In order to understand what a divorce with civility means for a couple, a look at the underlying marriage is helpful. Most people model their marriages after what they find familiar or comfortable, such as the marriage contract that existed between their parents, their friends or even a desired pattern of behavior from a favorite movie. Typically, the process of modeling is unconscious. The truth is that most people do not thoroughly consider the marriage before saying "I do" nor do they share with one another what their respective pictures of a successful marriage might look like. As a result, a good marriage with longevity is often an accident of fate or a result of trial and error where people learn what not to do from prior failed attempts.

Marriage education. Nowhere in the education curriculum is there a marriage course that offers play by play instruction or practical pointers on how to be successfully married. Priests, academics, doctors and sociologists have all broached the subject of marriage education, incorporating something to the effect of a marriage contract, but the idea of "how to" training for spouses is daunting and probably unreachable given the disparate variables at play. The idea of a "good marriage" is an amorphous concept as everyone has vastly differing views as to what constitutes a successful relationship. With respect to marriage education, it seems more sensible for the work to be done pre-marriage, with the focus on whether or not two individuals are compatible given their respective needs, wants, goals, and views. The ultimate relationship between two unique individuals is defined by the combination of many elements, experiences and characteristics and so really, there is no common denominator for a successful marriage.

The Relationship. While most people do not make an investment in pre-marital counseling other than what may be required, such as the mandated *Pre Cana* counseling offered by the Catholic Church, it is even more rare for people to give thought to an exit strategy prior to getting married, unless of course a prenuptial agreement is sought by one or both of the parties. Since by definition marriage is supposed to be "until death do us part," people are largely reluctant to consider that their marriage might otherwise end, despite the statistics. The truth is every marriage ends, the question is when. Will it be at death or before? A prenuptial agreement is entered into prior to the marriage and it typically sets out how the assets will be divided when the marriage ends at the time of death or divorce so that the resulting division is more favorable to the person seeking the agreement than that which would have occurred naturally according to the laws of the state where the parties live. Because discussing the end of the marriage before it begins is counterintuitive, to plan a wedding and a divorce at the same time, one party or both parties need to be strongly motivated to initiate such discussions. Additionally, since a prenuptial agreement can be expensive and time consuming, such an agreement is typically considered only by those who have significant assets going into the marriage, anticipate inheriting wealth at some point in the future, or have previously experienced a contentious divorce.

Ironically, exiting with dignity may be aided by an examination of how the couple came to enter this union in the first place. For some, it is helpful and in some instances crucial to understand the workings of the relationship before it can be civilly dismantled.

A graceful exit from a marriage requires a focus that capitalizes on the positives in the marriage, without rehashing all of the negatives or dwelling on that which did not work. To devise a scheme for a less painful exit, the identification of the positive aspects of the marriage may be helpful. Making a list of all of the positives in the marriage is a good way to start, but in order to do that one would be best served from starting at the beginning. What first attracted the partners? What interests did they share? What about the relationship was most enjoyable? What were the high points of the marriage? What was the model they had in mind at the onset of the marriage? How did the model of the parents of the parties factor into relationship? How did this marriage *positively* mirror that model?

Why the Attraction? Once the positive attributes are identified, it is helpful to identify that which was particularly attractive about this individual for the selection of him or her for marriage above all others. How did all this happen?

Examining what is often the only role model, one's parent's relationship, requires an honest look back. What was so pleasing or comfortable about that model to allow its incorporation into the blueprint for this marriage? If for example, one's parents were divorced, but prior to the divorce, the security of living in a tranquil home was the warm memory, then that very same tranquility, or the appearance of it, can become an unconscious goal; a positive image worthy of imitation. The problem is that people tend to imitate all that is familiar, including the negative pieces of our history. If, for example, the tranquility was marred by subsequent discord, that very entire pattern may be perpetuated. History translates to expectations; the old becomes the new again.

The marriage dance is developed over time on a foundation of expectations. The end of the marriage often comes when the unmet expectations exceed the met needs. It is the acknowledgement of those unmet expectations that may be required in order to move forward to the point of settlement of the divorce. Such acknowledgement can be accomplished through marital exit counseling with the help of a mental health professional and sometimes occurs within the context of mediation or even in discussions at four-way meetings, where the parties come together with respective counsel in an attempt to resolve the divorce issues. This acknowledgement or realization of what needs were unmet can also occur by simply taking the time to think the marriage through from start to finish, choosing in the end to appreciate the positives and let go of the negatives.

Future relationships. The rewards for facing how the marriage evolved not only helps pave the way for a less painful exit from the current relationship, but includes an insight into what may be required for subsequent relationships in order for them to succeed. So often, people leave one relationship with another already in the wings, tantamount to jumping from one moving iceberg to another. Time and thought are required to develop a process for avoiding another disaster similar to the failed marriage that has resulted in such pain and disappointment. In order to improve relationship success skills, one needs a contemplative period between relationships in order to truly appreciate what has worked and what has not and why. Some people believe they need, truly NEED someone close at hand all the time, like a blanket on a cold night. Yet, this inability to stand independently can in itself have a chilling effect on the missed opportunity to take a look at what, why and how things went wrong. Divorce, while an end, is also the chance to start anew, a chance to learn and grow, to develop new skills that won't allow a *pattern* of failed relationships to ensue. The pain in a divorce is often excruciating but if the experience is viewed as an opportunity for growth, then from the rubbles of the aftermath of the process, a plan can unfold to prevent the same events from reoccurring.

Time allows healing; healing allows for a second chance; a second chance that may be an opportunity to enjoy happiness. After a divorce, grieving for all that was lost needs to occur. That loss can be for the person, or for the security of the marriage or for the dashed expectations or for children, grandchildren or even in-laws. As grieving occurs, room becomes available for new interpersonal skills to be developed. The recuperative period after a divorce is an opportunity for reflection, emotional growth and for the psychological scars to heal.

Aside from all else, a soon divorce settlement is far more likely when the parties are not encumbered with the distraction of a new relationship while attempting to negotiate a resolution. Common sense dictates that the process works best if all remain focused on ending the old before ringing in the new. In addition, in terms of the next experience, an overlay of relationships is not helpful to either the terminating one or the germinating other.

If children are involved, the situation becomes even more complicated when there is an overlaying of a second relationship before the first has officially ended. Children need an opportunity to grieve, in most instances even more so than the parents. Many children believe that they are somehow at fault when a marriage between their parents fails to survive. The entire process becomes entangled when a third party is prematurely introduced into the equation, particularly when that third party is thrust upon the children, instantly infused into their lives. The children often become very confused by all of the unresolved emotional issues at work, and some simply shut down. They cannot accept the third party not only because they are not ready, but because their energies are still focused on their own personal losses. A child experiencing a divorce between his parents simply does not have the emotional capacity to all at once deal with the loss of his family, consider the needs of his parents, and accept strangers into his heart and life. In fact, there are few adults who could handle those expectations. Additionally, a child will often feel instantly disloyal when introduced to mom or dad's new friend. This entire process needs to be approached carefully and thoughtfully with a focus first on the child's acceptance of the divorce itself.

If the divorce spans years, then depending upon the child's healing process and reaction to the divorce, a child may possibly be ready to accept a third party before the process is finalized. However, under normal circumstances, in a divorce that encompasses a year or so, children need at least that amount of time to adjust to the changes that are occurring in their lives. As parents and spouses, no one would argue that the parties need an adjustment period. So too do the children. Everyone is seeking to redefine the shifting family shape to meet their own needs and there needs to be time to work out the dynamics of the immediate family members. A third party injected prematurely into the equation can unnaturally shorten the grieving process and the time required for the family to be restructured. As a reaction, children sometimes begin to act out or exhibit age inappropriate behavior.

Children only have one childhood. The courts are sensitive to the importance of minimizing disruption to the children's lives as much as possible, and issuing orders and judgments that will keep both parents in the children's lives. Typically, the courts attempt to follow the custodial blueprint the parties have created while the family was intact. However, a third party added prematurely to the mix can create havoc. A divorce is like a living entity and needs time to breath, evolve and process. All of the participants, especially the children experience at least some of the same stages of the grieving process that is experienced when a loved one dies. These stages ranging from anger to acceptance need to be experienced and simply cannot and should not be rushed. While adults may experience the process differently and require more or less time to readjust, children uniformly need room, time and breathing space to become accustomed to change. For children, a divorce is the recreation of the family unit from one group to two groups, with the rules of each often differing. It takes time for a child to become accustomed to these changes and it takes time for everything to settle into a secure and comfortable environment for them.

The process is totally beyond the control of a child. The divorce process *happens* to a child, while the adults actively participate to create what happens. Because in divorce, children are like corks on water, they need an opportunity to gain a foothold in what is happening to feel secure. One way to help their children is for the parents to behave rationally, reasonably, and like parents, not like children.

Some children perceive that they are responsible for the parent "left behind" when a third party is prematurely introduced. They become parentified. The child tries to take care of that parent who may be exhibiting outbursts of sadness, thus the child becomes the parent and the parent becomes the child. All this needs to be carefully sorted out as a child is a child only once and emotional damage suffered during those formative years is often impenetrable later in life.

Many people when experiencing a divorce are sincerely careful about their children; what they say in the presence of the children, to whom the children are introduced, and when and where such introductions take place. Nonetheless, children hold their emotional cards close to the chest during the process because they are simply on emotional overload, attempting to sort out more than anyone else involved. For a child, the entire world is shifting. Children study their parents. They study every move, every look. They dissect every word spoken. The reality is that divorce affects most children to the core and while most well-intentioned parents will say that the needs of the children come first, they often, under the stress of a divorce, begin to place their wants and needs before those of their children. It is common for judges to repeat the oft heard sentiment at the conclusion of a divorce hearing, "You may be spouses no longer, but you will always be the parents of your children." Take heed, stop and think. The future of your children depends on it.

The attraction and historical relationships. The blueprint of the past becomes the foundation for the present for those who have inherited dysfunctional behaviors from their parents. For example, for a child of an alcoholic parent, alcohol is a significant component of his or her historical environment and an unconscious familiar backdrop allowing continued exposure to alcoholic behavior to serve as a comfort zone. Because of the familiarity, a child of an alcoholic is more likely to enter into a relationship with an abusive drinker simply because the environment is a familiar one. Even though an adult child of an alcoholic may vow to never be in a relationship with a gross and confirmed alcoholic, that same person may have a tendency to dismiss or minimize the signals of a heavy drinker. The child of an alcoholic positively interprets the behavior of the popular person who drinks too much as positive rather than as a warning or a negative. The very quality that should be a warning sign is instead comfortable.

While the characteristics of dysfunctional alcohol abuse are identifiable and specific, this analogy can be applied to any dysfunctional behavior by which children are affected. Such a less obvious behavior could be reflected by a partner who freely offers "constructive" criticism during the courtship phase. Initially, the family history might condition one to dismiss such critical remarks with a justification that the other person is smarter and superior than he or she is, or somehow means well. The potential spouse's criticism might be construed as helpful with an unconscious expectation that such superior knowledge may have future value in the journey of life. The historical experience from the critical parent acts to cloud the potentially emotionally damaging blows from the critical partner for a while. However, once married and confronted with daily criticisms which ultimately evolve into reminders of ones own inferiority and the other's superiority, the situation can become unbearable. Ultimately, the criticized spouse's self worth diminishes to the point where nothing appears to be adequate.

With most traits perceived as having value in the beginning, a price is paid later. If the marriage works out, then a reconciliation occurs between the positive and negative; there is acceptance. If the marriage ends in divorce, either the negatives outweigh the positives, or the unmet expectations exceed the met expectations. For a graceful and reasonable exit, the parties both need to be able to let go of all of this.

In the beginning of the relationship, the attraction is enjoyed without consideration of the cost. For example, a divorce from a highly trained professional such as a doctor may be a case in point. While the doctor spouse may have been an attractive prospect as a mate, little or no appreciation may have been originally given to the effect of the many years of solitude in study to become a doctor, which may have resulted in a history of undeveloped or neglected interpersonal relationship skills. When the couple gets together initially in the glow of the future security and financial possibilities, no time is taken to explore the "price" of the years of academic focus and isolation, during which the individual puts aside all else but his or her professional preparation.

As the professional begins to evolve socially into a very different person than who existed at the onset of the marriage, the response might be that "this is not the person I married." Divorces with this scenario can often be the most acrimonious because the initial marriage contract appeared to have such promise that the level of expectation becomes unrealistic. The greater the expectations the greater the disappointment when those expectations are not met. Since marriage is a contract of expectations, when a contract is broken, there is disappointment and often resentment and anger.

Problems arise when one spouse believes that the basis for the bargain is one thing and the other spouse believes it to be another. As always, when the participants' expectations do not mesh or fall short, conflict results. Injecting love and titillation into the equation, the final chapter may be difficult to unravel.

Foiled expectations are the stuff of divorce. Misspoken expectations are the blueprint for a failed marriage. In the divorce, the anger and disillusionment erupts. The more people are wedded to their unmet expectations the more difficult it is to reach an agreement. For some that end comes on the steps of the courthouse, on the day of trial or even after a costly drawn out trial. However, in mediation, a graceful exit can transpire before one's financial and emotional capital is totally exhausted.

Since every couple is unique, the process to resolve the divorce is not the same for everyone. Communication, even if initially loud and raucous, is critical. It is often the unspoken expectation that is at the core of the divide. The hidden agenda or engines that drive the anger to a fever pitch may include lack of appreciation of contribution, constant criticism which is the death by a thousand cuts, or sarcasm which goes to the core of self worth. It is not until the hidden agenda is at least recognized in some measure can the divorce be resolved.

A four-way meeting with the participants and their attorneys with or without a mediator is often helpful. An experienced divorce attorney can help to diffuse and acknowledge such hidden agenda; on the other hand, an attorney who adopts the client's hidden agenda can deepen and widen the divide especially if that attorney acts from the belief that every case needs to be tried. While typically most attorneys do not take this view, with an extremely angry or entitled client, an attorney might be convinced to adopt such an agenda, thus making it even more difficult for the parties to reach settlement. When the party successfully finds an ally in anger, the attorney, it is almost impossible to resolve things amicably as the voice of reason is absent. Even in this instance, mediation or collaborative law techniques can go a long way to reduce some of this tension which prevents settlement if the participant open to the possibility.

Even with an angry litigant and an aggressive attorney, an avenue of settlement may still be pursued if the more reasonable spouse is willing to approach the angry spouse to discuss the issues in mediation or in the presence of a mental health professional who is savvy enough decipher the hidden agendas at play. Sometimes, the angry litigant simply wants an apology, not empty words, but a heartfelt acknowledgement of the real or imagined wrongdoing perpetuated by the other spouse. In mediation, for example, even if a couple is disposed toward settlement, the process may begin smoothly but be marked by turbulence later. As emotions surface, sometimes parties become committed to resolution of the financial portion of their marriage, but only if the "truth" is told about the third party. In Massachusetts, communications that occur during mediation sessions are typically confidential and therefore, such sharing can freely occur because admissions cannot usually be used in court. In some instances, until such time as responsibility for the fault leading to the ending of the marriage is accepted and the parties are emotionally set free, finality can not result. While the concept of fault, in most states, is not a major consideration, some still need to be acknowledged as wronged before they can effectively move on. Fault often becomes the unspoken agenda blocking any possibility for resolution.

Another common problem in divorce is the detrimental influence of family members of one or both parties. If one partner is still in love with the other, but a parent's dislike of a spouse creates divided allegiances, the results is much like with the interference caused by extramarital relationships. Family members can be a toxic ingredient, not only in the marriage, but also in the divorce.

In open court, after listening to a mother exhaust her venom about her "worthless" son in law, who in her estimation did not support her daughter in the style to which she was accustomed, the Judge finally said, "Has it ever occurred to you, that had you left them alone and to their own devices to sink or swim, they would have been fine?" Presumably, the Judge's comments provided enough of an acknowledgement for the couple to come to an agreement and move on with their lives. It is fair to assume that in the end, what was blocking the settlement was not a financial issue or anything related to the divorce, but a faulty marriage contract that included a toxic third party.

For some issues, assistance from a mental health professional is helpful. For example, gambling is perhaps a difficult if not impossible barrier to successful relationships, as gambling is not only a vice, but often a symptom of a personality disorder. Such an addiction may also be the manifestation of bipolar disorder, with an attractive face early on, with little possibility of cure without serious commitment and/or medication. By definition, the gambler is not attracted to cleaning up his or her act. In terms of ending a marriage to a gambler, the other spouse is as much an enabler as the spouse of an alcoholic, therefore the acknowledgement of the addiction to gambling is central to the process, but most difficult to achieve. While in a divorce, the objective is to sever the relationship, the dance between the gambler and the enabler sometimes adds to the challenges of achieving an amicable resolution.

Chapter III

And Baby Makes Three

Irrespective of whether a child is conceived after careful consideration and discussion or by way of an "accident," the birth of a child causes the marital relationship to be irrevocably altered. The relationship may become better or worse, but it is always changed by the addition of a child, if for no other reason than that the needs of third person being become central to the marriage and sometimes those needs override the needs of the marital partners.

Child care becomes a self defining role for some people who may have entered the marriage with the preconceived notion that he or she would be a stay at home parent when the time came, no matter what. Frequently it is this issue that can begin to break down the marital relationship. This is true especially if one spouse feels that the role of child care should be full time only for a limited period of time or simply does not value the role, seeing it as a part-time role to be supplemented by a part-time paying job, or less important employment than that of a primary wage earner. This is a juncture at which the parties often engage in a dance of positioning to realign their relationship and expectations after a child is born.

The role of child care becomes an especially problematic if the child has exceptional needs, such as emotional or physical problems that may warrant full time attention by one of the parties. Given that the parties become understand-ably concerned with the child's struggles, they typically do not have the emotional wherewithal to focus on anything but the child. A sick or special needs child is not usually a possibility contemplated prior to marriage. Absent intensive and effective communication, the circumstances of the family are so seriously altered by such an unforeseen circumstance that the irretriev-able breakdown of the marriage often becomes inevitable. The wage earner of the marriage may respond by essentially aban-doning the parenting effort, entirely putting the responsibility of the child on the primary care parent's shoulders. When this happens, the bitterness and blame game heightens to a level of acrimony that is difficult to penetrate.

Often, the custodial parent is armed with family support, which can exacerbate the family fissure, because the family whispers to the custodial parent all the reasons the other spouse is WRONG for not offering more hands-on support. The family begins to be a part of the breakdown agenda since they shoulder part of the load the WRONG spouse is supposed to shoulder. In a sense, the marriage becomes a triangle with each parent and the child in a standoff. The reality is that the marriage becomes destroyed by the onslaught of an unforeseen event that neither party included in their contract of expec-tations. Therefore new expectations develop, which are hardly ever negotiated between the couple. It is truly a miracle when a couple is able to renegotiate the marriage and survive as a couple in the face of a sick child.

Parenting Plan. Most spouses have shared or joint legal custody which means that they jointly make the major reli-gious, education and medical decisions together. Despite that, the children typically live with one parent or the other, and that parent makes the day to day decisions. That parent becomes the physical custodian. People can also agree to have shared legal and shared physical custody with the children spending half their time with each parent, such as alternate weeks, or three days with one and four with the other, on a rotating basis. However, shared legal and shared physical custody requires an extraordinary commitment on the part of the parties to communicate well with one another, reside nearby and share all of the financial and other responsibilities of child rearing. Such an arrangement is rare, since if the parties are able to communicate to this degree, in most instances they would not be in a divorce situation in the first place. Therefore, most arrangements are for the parties to have shared legal custody and one parent to have physical custody, while the non-custodial parent has parenting time, commonly known as visitation.

If the parties cannot agree to a parenting schedule, then the court will impose one, which is often alternate weekends and one night a week for dinner for the non custodial parent to see and take the children and the parties sharing major holidays.

The rules governing which parent is granted custody or the custodial allocation is gender neutral. As a practical matter, the courts look as what the historical arrangement has been between the parties with respect to the care of the children. If one spouse has been the homemaker and caretaker for the children, the courts take that into consideration in an attempt to least upset the arrangement to which the children are accustomed. However, in this day, the role of homemaker is often defined as part-time once the children reach school age. With the ever increasing need for two full-time incomes in a household, the typical two parent family with children consists of both parties making regular contributions to the role of homemaker as well as financially. Nonetheless the courts continue to look to that parent who has primarily fulfilled the role of primary caretaker to the children to continue in such a role post-divorce as the primary physical custodian. The court will want to hear who stayed home with them when they were small, who made the doctors appointments, who attended such appointments, who principally interfaced with the schools, who was in charge of day care, who was basically in charge of the children.

In order to retain control over the parenting arrangements after the separation and divorce, it is critical that parties commit to working together for the purpose of devising their own comprehensive, personal parenting plan that is feasible for all involved. Effectively, once the courts become involved in the lives of a family with children, the children theoretically become wards of the state and the state then parcels back to the parents their parental rights and assigns responsibilities, such as support. For example, with shared legal custody, the parties may have the right to jointly make major medical, religious and educational decisions together but if they cannot communicate, the court will decide which parent will have that responsibility. In order for the system to work, the state steps in and defines the parents' roles in their children's lives. When there is a breakdown in communication between the parents, the court steps in and becomes the supreme parent, organizing the children's lives as well as the lives of the parents.

The most usual court orders are in the form of a parenting plan which sets out when the children spend time with each parent. It is better for people to make these decisions themselves, reduce the plan to writing for the court to review and accept, which it typically does (An example of such a plan is appended hereto). This parenting plan should be negotiated separate and apart from financial considerations. A best start point is to prepare a proposed plan which is detailed and includes all of the vacations, religious holidays and periodic and weekly parenting time such as that which is in the appendix of this book. A non specific plan which gives the non custodial parent reasonable visitation with reasonable notice, may work for awhile, but typically as time goes on, it is prone to fail. Each party has the right to make a life and schedule which includes the children. A non specific arrangement leaves room for misunderstandings and unmet expectations. Problems especially result when third parties are introduced into a parent's life, since often that individual will also have scheduling needs as well. Such issues are even more challenging when the significant other also has children or when a parent and second spouse has a child, at which point the scheduling of the parenting time for a blended family may become even more complicated. As a result, that specific parenting plan with designated times for exchange of the children, as well as very specific holiday scheduling works best in the long run. By doing this, a fall back position is established in the divorce agreement, and while it may be modifiable as time goes on, at least the plan is in place should the communication break down. The schedule becomes the basis for each parent to make employment related plans, vacation arrangements, social commitments and child related events.

The optimum way to proceed would be with the couple themselves talking about what they want in the plan. Although such communication may be difficult, the parties should at least make an attempt. The attorneys are not going to be there every time the plan needs to be revised. In addition, this exercise is helpful because the parents need to develop an ability to discuss what is best for the children. When the relationship between the parents works well, they should ultimately be able to adjust the parenting schedule as needed. It does, however, make life easier for all involved for there to be at least a basic visitation schedule in place.

What is reasonable? Since children only have so much waking time, consideration needs to be given to the age appropriate commitments the children may have. It is unrealistic for a parenting plan to be put in place for a seventeen year old, but even for a ten year old who has athletic, academic and social events, the parents need to balance the child's activities and the parenting time. This sometimes become difficult if a parent takes the position that every moment of the child's life needs to be mapped out without taking into consideration the child's need to have some free time. This aspect of the divorce agreement requires thoughtful negotiation and consideration in order to design the most effective and acceptable arrangement for all involved without parceling out every minute. In order to have a civil exit from a marriage, the best approach for devising a parenting plan is to take an honest look at the child's life as it existed when the family was intact. The pattern is easily apparent in the life of a teenager, who has long hours for homework, a part time job on the weekends, and even when the parties were together, spent little time with them. Amazingly with such a situation, some feuding parents still attempt to allocate the teenager's time, rather than allowing their respective parenting time to flow along the lines of what is age appropriate.

Even though every parenting plan needs to be tailored to both the parents' needs as well as the child's needs and schedule, a parent's ability to consider the welfare of their child does far more in the long run to foster his or her relationship with the child. A parent clinging to each precious minute rather than yielding to some arrangement that is flexible and in concert with a child's needs will ultimately backfire and can cause that child to become resentful, resulting in strained parent-child interactions. The relationship can deteriorate to the point where sometimes the children become so unforgiving that the net result can be a total breakdown where there is absolutely no relationship at all. Parents must consider the long term consequences to unrealistic and selfish demands. On the other hand, interference frustrating visitation and custody arrangements can backfire to alienate the interfering custodial parent. Even if such tactics are rewarded with "success" in that the child stops visiting the other parent, the harm to the child is inestimable in the long run.

Once a parent agrees to spend certain time with the child, predetermined parenting time needs to be an absolute priority. Failure to show up for visitation or chronic lateness, even with reason, is painful for a child. At the same time, making alternate plans for the child who is scheduled to be with the other parent is undermining, disrespectful and can ultimately backfire.

Depending upon the age and disposition of the child, a parent arriving late for a visitation with or without prior communication can be interpreted by the child in a variety of ways, none of which are positive for the child or for the parents. Children love both parents usually and they do not want to take sides. They desire time with both parents even if they have input into the selection of the custodial parent. I once had a teenage child approach me to inquire if I could sue his non custodial mother to force her to visit him. The pain children suffer in divorce is immeasurable.

Winning for the sake of winning in terms of a parenting plan is a lose-lose situation. Sometimes less time is more, especially for older children. In a divorce, the parents are not only renegotiating their own relationships, but the parents are renegotiating their relationships with their children. A demand for custody when the bottom line is to use the children as a negotiating tool to force the other party to do something such as drop the divorce action, or accept a lower support payment is an oft seen maneuver which throws the children into a tail spin. Even seeking custody when clearly the other party has historically been the primary parent, and continues to be the primary parent, is using the children to gain an advantage. The operative phrase is "using the children." While under ordinary circumstances a parent would never hurt a child, in divorce, for some folks, all bets are off and nothing is sacred. The worst infraction is parental alienation which is where one parent alienates the children from the other as part of the divorce. Such a tactic is tantamount to abuse where one parent uses the children to punish and control the other parent.

The word civility is not just applicable to one's spouse, but is also applicable to one's children. Such civility includes putting the children ahead of a new, blossoming relationship with a significant, or sometime insignificant, other. This means visiting with the children alone and not creating a blended family when the old family is not yet redefined by divorce. Even once the divorce is final, spending at least some alone time with the children is an important investment for all. Even the other spouse may also appreciate seeing the children adjust to the new arrangement. With divorce, everything is new by definition.

A custodial parent needs to abide by the same rules as the non custodial parent, spending some alone time with each child. Each child needs to be treated as special. This approach can go a long way to not only meeting children's needs, but to communicating to the other spouse that the children's needs are first. A divorce can be a positive wake up call for individuals to become aware of parental shortcomings giving that parent a second chance to become a better parent after a divorce than they were before the divorce.

Effective exit communication not only includes reasonably discussing relevant divorce issues, but taking appropriate actions and exhibiting respectful behavior towards children. It is imperative that the parents be able to talk and not scream at one another or even be sarcastic, in the presence of the children. Some children become so devastated that they try to kill themselves. Children between the ages of five and seven are in my experience the most vulnerable. At these ages, the children don't understand what they hear and do not have the maturity to separate themselves in any way, thus they believe they are the cause for the fighting and the divorce. While parents do not intend to hurt their children, the byproduct of their behavior in their children's presence is by definition hurtful.

On the other hand, children are aware of more than their parents credit them. It is not uncommon for a young child to wonder why he doesn't have what everyone else in his class has, i.e. a divorce. Additionally, it is not uncommon for a child to wonder not if but when his parents are getting a divorce. Children are savvy; they watch television and go to the movies. They talk about divorce with their friends. The real issue is what do they say about YOUR divorce? How can a parent better deal with a child's reaction to divorce? The parent's calm communication and unified parenting front pays dividends in the long run in a child's life.

Some school systems have support groups for children in divorcing or divorced families. It is always a good idea for the parents to advise the schools of any major custodial shifts or issues surrounding the divorce process so that educators and school counselors can best address the needs of the child.

Chapter IV

Assets and income

Disclosure. The courts have a philosophy of open book discovery, which in short means that you need to fully disclose all of your finances and assets to the other side and to the court. It is interesting that during the courtship phase of marriage, in a traditional relationship, the "he" often picks up the tab while the "she" often graciously accepts. During the dissolution of a marriage, that sentiment changes. The reality is that the sooner everyone "fesses up" to what they each have, the sooner the case is in a position to settle and reach an end.

The participants in a divorce have had an intermingling of funds and assets to one degree or another. It may be that not every asset will be divided equally or even at all if the terms of a prenuptial agreement governs, but full disclosure is usually mandated just the same.

Where there is lack of full disclosure, suspicion and distrust results. Consequently, suspicion and distrust lead to increased legal fees, because attorneys must "dig" to find assets. It is that very suspicion and distrust that gives rise to untold anger, not only in reaction to the exaggerated legal costs, but because parties feel that they may potentially be cheated out of what, in their estimation, is rightfully due. The unwillingness to be forthright fuels concerns about an unjust result.

While the lack of disclosure altogether is an issue, the

lack of speedy disclosure is equally as troublesome and can be as costly. To receive information in piecemeal is frustrating to the waiting party. Providing current information in an open manner as quickly and as often as possible engenders good will and fuels the belief that the negotiations will be above board and honest.

Cutting up the pie. One of the worst aspect of asset division is when people attach a sentiment to certain property, which is disproportionate to the value of that property, due to the "but that is MINE" attitude. For example, an actual divorce case went to trial simply because the wife refused to give the husband his two hundred dollar watch. Another like case was heard because the parties could not to their mutual satisfaction divide an inexpensive doll collection. In cases such as these. In cases such as these, any person thinking rationally would realize that the cost of trial is going to far exceed the value of the assets at issue. The war is really not about the asset, but about a secret agenda both litigants are harboring; one for insisting upon the asset and the other for refusing the asset.

Another emotional issue is the custody of household pets. While people can understandably feel very passionately about their pets, they need to make every attempt to reach a resolution before asking counsel to present the same to a judge, since the court is not equipped to resolve such disputes nor is the court interested. An annoyed judges does not benefit anyone.

Appreciating the value of assets or animals is not enough; the division needs to occur. Occasionally, one might include a visitation schedule for the dog or horse, or a provision that the house not get sold until the cat dies. Admittedly, there are those occasions when seemingly trivial matters become insurmountable, as in the case of the watch. At a time such as this, it is imperative for the involved persons to do some soul searching, seek the advice of a mental health counselor or defer to the advice of his or her attorney. Another bitter divorce was one of a marriage that lasted for two weeks. Again, soul searching, counseling, and/or deferring to counsel could have avoided such a train wreck. And split they did. Incredulously, the aftermath of this short lived, virtually non-existent marriage, was a divorce that went on for a year during which this couple battled over the wedding gifts. Again, soul searching, counseling, and/or deferring to counsel could have avoided such a train wreck.

An infamous local divorce court story revolved around a dispute about who should be granted a novelty plastic toilet seat cover. This toilet seat was the subject of a bitter and presumably expensive fight, unbelievable as that may be.

While the reader may think these examples are in jest, sadly they are now all part of court records since they were aired in open court before the public for all to hear. Any divorce attorney who has been around the bend for a day or two can recite similar war stories of cases they have also heard while waiting for their client's case to be called. Some cases can make one's hair prickle at the waste of precious time The avoidable pain experienced by people due to irrational fighting over nominally valued items, expending thousands in legal fees to process the fight, is perhaps one of the most frustrating components of litigated divorces. At the same time, attorneys need to be willing to point out to a client when his or her demands are irrational or simply not feasible. In these instances, the fight is not about the asset but is a reaction to the disappointment of those failed, unnamed, unacknowledged expectations. Name the expectations that have not been met; acknowledge the disappointment, and commit to moving past both.

Chapter V

Attorneys and the Judicial System

The Attorney. In order to become an attorney, an individual needs to graduate from college, complete law school, and pass a bar examination specific to the state where he or she hopes to practice. Additionally, most states require attorneys to pass an ethical examination. The process is arduous and challenging. Qualities and qualifications most important in choosing a divorce attorney are ethics, experience, and responsiveness to client's needs. A person must be comfortable with his chosen counsel, believing that his or her attorney is not only able to meet his or her needs, but is also able to clearly explain the process while willing to take the time to answer questions along the way.

The attorney is licensed to dispense advice or speak on behalf of people to advance their position. Family Law is a specific area, which requires an extensive knowledge of the law and demands patience. There is an accepted maxim among lawyers that the difference between a criminal litigant and divorce litigant is that the criminal litigant is on his or her best behavior during the process while the divorce client is on his or her worst behavior. A good divorce lawyer will refer the client to a competent therapist or at least suggest therapy during the process, as the unavoidable stress of a divorce has been seen to have untold physical and emotional effects on people. The more emotionally healthy a client is, the easier it is to settle the case. It is realistic to expect the attorney to return client calls within a reasonable period of time or if the attorney is in court or otherwise engaged, for someone from the office to respond. It is also realistic for the attorneys to return phone calls to opposing counsel. It is reasonable to expect to have a meeting at some time with the attorneys and both parties, in an effort to resolve the divorce, and arrive at a meeting of minds regarding the divorce. The purpose of this communication is to receive and send the required information, assemble that information into some reasonable way to begin to bring the divorce to conclusion. If the divorce cannot be concluded by the time these meetings take place, the courts will have a hearing to make recommendations for settlement, so that the process can move towards settlement.

A divorce mediator should also have experience in divorce related cases and mediations, be ethical and have an ability to explain. Legal training for a divorce mediator is helpful, but specifically marital divorce experience is particularly important since the practice of divorce law requires not only skill and knowledge but the ability to understand how to assist parties.

The Legal Process. Most divorce settlements are negotiated once the discovery phase of the process is completed. Discovery is the exchange of all of the financial documents required by the court or by way of discovery requests made between the parties, to accurately identify the assets and determine the value thereof.

If attempts at settlement are unsuccessful, a trial date is set and, at great expense, the court will hear the particulars of the case as required by the law of the State which has the jurisdiction and a judgment will ultimately be entered. At the time of trial, the judge will hear the testimony of each of the parties, sometimes that of friends and family, as well as expert testimony of real estate appraisers and or business appraisers if values of the marital assets are contested. All testimony is given in court open to the public, for anyone and everyone to hear. One of the advantages to settlement aside from the exorbitant costs of preparation of each witness is that it allows parties to retain their privacy. The costs can be disproportionate to value of the dispute, since once the preparation commences, the attorneys are duty bound to present all of the relevant evidence and to rebut the testimony presented by the opposing spouse, if it is appropriate to dispute.

Lastly, once a trial begins, the litigants lose control over the outcome, and testimony which may sound predictable in an attorney's office may veer down a very different path once at trial and subject to cross-examination, even with careful preparation. A trial leaves the life decisions of the family in the hands of a judge who hears testimony within the context of his or her life. One of the most persuasive reasons to settle is to be able to have input into the outcome. Once the decision is in the hands of a judge, the litigants no longer have an opportunity to give that input except via written submissions to the judge for a suggested judgment or findings, which may or may not be adopted.

Aside from the cost, control over the family is relinquished to a third party about whom the litigants know little. The parties must assume that the judge is capable of making better major life decisions than they are able to make for themselves. The judge decides the destiny of people who are unable to sit down together to design a plan for their family and while that notion may offer warring couples some sense of relief, whereby they do not need to do it all themselves, it is important the people realize the broad discretion available to a judge. Going to trial is ultimately rolling the dice and although there are some safeguards in place within the judicial system, the reality is that trying a case as opposed to settling it is always a gamble.

Judges are either appointed by the Governor or elected by the people depending on the laws of the state. Additionally, divorce laws are also determined by the government of the state in which the parties reside and each state has different laws and rules for a divorce. However, as a universal principal, if all else fails, the judicial system is designed to resolve a dispute by rendering a decision after hearing the evidence and the witnesses. The process could be lengthy if the trial is contested, meaning that there is a lack of agreement on the terms of the divorce, or in some states where a divorce on the grounds of "no fault" is not available, the court will decide whether or not the court is empowered to grant a divorce. In a state that does not offer "no fault" as an option, the court needs to determine whether there is sufficient fault to grant a divorce. Most states grant a divorce whether or not either party is at fault.

Most cases have the potential to settle; that is, reach resolution absent court intervention. It is only the rare case that needs to be tried, such as where a point of law is not clear. The reason a case does not settle is usually because someone is unreasonable. With experienced attorneys, and the availability of alternative dispute resolution, even the most difficult case should be resolved if the parties and their counsel are willing to put in the time and energy to come to a consensus. Often the block to settlement is an unarticulated agenda on the part of one party, or an unwillingness to spend the time to communicate and effectuate a resolution. Appreciating that no process is more emotional than a divorce, the participants if guided with reasonable options, should be able to come to a consensus if they are willing.

A pretrial conference is a court date with the judge, both litigants and their attorneys set prior to a trial date, and with an agenda for the Court to offer some guidance providing options for settlement. While settlement assistance from a good judge is invaluable, the burden to settle a case remains with the parties and their attorneys. The parties need to attend the pre trial conference with a solid understanding of the issues at hand, and their respective positions on the issues. Attorneys need to prepare a comprehensive pre trial memorandum, laying out the status of the case and the potential for settlement, giving the client an opportunity to review and fully understand the document prior to it being filed with the Court. Attorneys should also have at least the framework of a proposed Agreement started and reviewed with the client prior to the pre trial so that a client has the opportunity to give some input and help guide his or her own case toward settlement. An attorney is duty bound to ensure that his or her client understands each and every word of these documents and this should occur prior to the pre trial. Expending valuable court time, or time that could be utilized for the purpose of settlement negotiations, to explain a document to one's own client is wasteful and counterproductive. The operative word is preparation.

Chapter VI

After the Divorce

Children. If children are involved in a divorce, some aspects of the divorce are never final until those children are considered emancipated (no longer dependent) and even after that, the parties through their children will remain somewhat connected. As a matter of practicality, divorced spouses are called upon by their children to together attend graduations, celebrate weddings, commemorate various religious event points, become grandparents, etc. Thus, that tenuous thread of connection perseveres. The children played an important role in the marriage and will play an equally important role in the divorce. It is therefore paramount that parties consider the children, their needs, and their feelings all the way through.

While all parents must continually balance the needs of the children with their own, this matter becomes significantly more complicated when parents divorce. While a divorced parent may need and deserve to start a new life after the divorce, the process has the capacity to have immeasurable long term effects on the children, particularly when children are prematurely introduced to parents' new significant others. The manner by which a third party is interjected into the life of a child is critical and can affect everyone's ability to enjoy a harmonious family life thereafter. As such, these types of introductions should occur very slowly with children's reactions carefully considered step by step.

Likewise, taking the time and effort to become acquainted with the former spouse's significant other is a difficult but important step given that the children will ultimately spend time with this individual. Rather than likening the former spouse to *Attila the Hun* and giving into the tendency to criticize and condemn, it may make more sense to extend the olive branch in an effort to calm the waters for the benefit of all involved, most of all the children. There are truly only a few instances where such magnanimity is impossible.

Moving on does not mean that every person in the former spouse's life needs to be an enemy. While one may understandably never be particularly chummy with a former spouse and his or her new love, there is rarely cause for feuding or posturing. In fact, these individuals can be allies in meeting the needs of the children. A certain level of harmony between divorced spouses and their respective mates will do wonders in terms of best meeting the needs of the children.

The notion of civility does not mean rolling over dead and acquiescing to anything offered, no matter how inappropriate. Rather civility means viewing what's on the table as a possibility and a willingness to take a look at how it affects the children. Civility means thinking outside the box. The emotional toll of a divorce on the parties is mammoth, no question, but that toll is undeniably worse for the children. The children did not ask to come into this world but were conceived and invited by parents who have a continued obligation to guarantee that they are safe, happy, cared for and educated, irrespective of the state of a marriage.

The standard in most states for the determination of

custody is best interests of the children. Putting the children's needs above one's own desire for revenge and retaliation is the best example of meeting those best interests. Acid corrodes the vessel. The anger and hate that is often so evident during a divorce will, in most cases, diffuse over time but after inestimable damage to the parties and the children. Ideally, parties should work toward diffusing it sooner rather than later, during the process so that a resolution can proceed more quickly, less painfully, and less expensively. Parties need to choose civility.

Civility. Civility, while a simple concept, can also become a state of mind if so chosen. The variables of any given relationship are infinite, so too are the numbers of opportunities to act civilly toward another human being, whether that human being is a stranger on the street or your soon to be ex-spouse. Unkindness introduced into any situation will not improve things; it can only escalate and further complicate a matter. Individuals in the unfortunate throes of a divorce must find the means and motivation to adopt civility as the state of mind. If entrusting in the notion of civility for the benefit of an individual who was once important to you is not a sufficient motivator, then perhaps focusing on the good it will serve you or your children will guide your course.

Many divorce cases can be described as beyond acrimonious, but even in those situations, a relentlessly angry spouse will usually reach the limit where the exhaustion and pain of the fight has taken its toll and the acrimony must finally end. In almost all cases there comes a point where people are simply ready to move on. In all cases, a divorce will be entered, property will be divided, and the custody of the children will be resolved. With those inevitabilities on the horizon, there is no sense in prolonging the emotional and financial agony when there is clearly another, more humane avenue by which the same end can be reached. After three decades of participating in countless divorces, the most persuasive benefit I can offer for choosing a divorce with civility is to simply say that it is, by far and without question, the better way for all involved.

APPENDIX

SAMPLE VISITATION SCHEDULE

Mid-Week:

It is the intention of the parties that both parents will be integrally involved with the life of the child on a daily basis is possible. However, the parties are cognizant of the realities of life, and have agreed that the Wife will move to the xxxxx area, but that additional moves for the child shall be discussed before such move so as not to remove the child unnecessarily from either party's access and so that both parties may have input into the educational opportunities to which the child may avail himself in the town in which he lives and school system in which his enrolled.

When the child is in school:

The Father shall have alternating weekend visitation with the children, every other Friday at 5:00 p.m. to Sunday at 5:00 p.m., unless there is a Monday holiday in which event, the Father will return the child on Monday at 5:00 P.M. with transportation to be shared equally by the parties.

During the week, Father shall have visitation with the minor child twice per week, on days to be agreed upon, from

5:00 P.M. to 8:00 P.M. with transportation to be provided by the Father.

When the child is not in school:

The Father shall have alternating weekend visitation with the children, every other Friday at 5:00 p.m. to Sunday at 5:00 p.m., unless there is a Monday holiday in which event, the Father will return the child on Monday at 5:00 P.M. with transportation to be shared equally by the parties.

During the week, Father shall have over-night visitation with the minor child twice per week, for two consecutive days from 5:00 P.M. through the second day at 5:00 P.M. with transportation to be shared equally by the parties.

Vacations:

If Mother intends to be out of town, Father will be allowed custody of the minor children during the time that Mother is away. Likewise, if Father intends to be out of town, the Mother shall be allowed custody of the minor children during the time that Father is away.

Each party shall have two (2) weeks uninterrupted summer vacation with the children during the year. The Father shall notify the Mother of his vacation schedule by May 1st for the up and coming summer in Odd years. The Mother shall notify the Father of her vacation scheduled by May 15th for the up and coming summers in Odd years, taking time that the Father has not selected. In even years, this arrangement shall be flip flopped.

Each week shall commence at 5:00 p.m. on a Friday through the second Sunday thereafter at 5:00 p.m. During each of the scheduled vacations with the children, the vacationing parent shall both pick up and drop off the children.

School Vacations:

February Vacation:
Odd years with Father and Even years with Mother.

April Vacation:
Odd years with Mother and Even years with Father.
Each week shall commence at 5:00 p.m. on a Friday through the second Sunday thereafter at 5:00 p.m. During each of the scheduled vacations with the children, the vacationing parent shall both pick up and drop off the children.

Christmas Vacation: Each party shall have one half of the Christmas school vacation, with the Mother having the first half in all Odd years and the Father having the first half in all Even years. The first half shall commence at 12:00 noon on December 26th through 5:00 p.m. on December 29th; the second half shall commence at 5:00 p.m. on December 29th through New Year's Day (January 1st) at 5:00 p.m.

Easter: Commences 4:00 p.m. on the Saturday before Easter through 5:00 p.m. Easter Sunday.
Odd years with Mother and Even Years with Father.

Mother's Day: The Children are always with Mother, commencing 10:00 a.m. on Mother's Day. If Mother's Day falls on the Father's weekend, this day shall <u>not</u> be made up on another weekend. If the Father has visitation, he shall bring the children to the Mother's home.

Father's Day: The Children are always with Father commencing 10:00 a.m. on Father's Day through 5:00 p.m. on Father's Day. If Father's Day falls on Mother's weekend, this day shall <u>not</u> be made up on another weekend. If the Mother has visitation, she shall bring the children to the Father's home, the Father shall return the children at 5:00 p.m.

Fourth of July: Commences 9:00 a.m. on July 4th through 5:00 p.m. on July 5th.
Even years with the Father and Odd years with the Mother.

Halloween (evening): Commencing 4:00 p.m. to be returned home by 8:00 p.m. by the Father, or Mother if Halloween falls within Father's visitation.
Even years with Mother; Odd years with Father.

Thanksgiving: Commences 9:00 a.m. Thanksgiving Day through 5:00p.m. the Friday after Thanksgiving.
Odd years with Mother, Even years with Father.

Christmas: Commences 12:00 noon on Christmas Eve, through 12:00 noon on Christmas Day.
Odd years with Father and Even years with Mother.
Christmas Day commencing 12:00 noon through December 26th at 12:00 noon.
Odd years with Mother and Even years with Father.

Additional 3-day weekends: Whoever is scheduled to have the child on the Saturday/Sunday of these weekends shall keep the child on the Monday holiday as well, until 5:00 p.m. However, if Father is working on the Monday holiday, he shall return the child by 5:00 p.m. on Sunday:

Miscellaneous:

Child's Birthdays: The child's birthday shall be spent with whichever parent has the child. The other parent shall have the right to call the child on his birthday.

Child's Activities: This Agreement and the visitation will supersede all the child's activities unless the parties agree in advance to activities which may fall on the other parent's weekend, in which event both parents will be obligated to take the child to such activities.

Each parent shall have reasonable telephone access to the child during the other's visitation periods.

Alternating weekends shall continue after an interrupted holiday or vacation visit as if the holiday or vacation never occurred.